Publish A Book

A Manual for Writers

How to Write, Market & Publish Your First Bestseller

25+ Tips and Tricks to Write Non Fiction Books, Research Papers, Theses, and Dissertations

By Zach Raymond

Description

There are countless writers out there, all writing for different reasons. Some write for work, others write for school, and still others are aspiring writers just waiting for their big break into the world of literature.

No matter what the reason is for the writing, there is a common thread that pulls them all together. All writers seek to be good at what they do.

Are you one of these writers? Do you have a dream of publishing a great non fiction book? Or are you a student that has been challenged to write a research paper or thesis to make or break your grade?

Are you digging deep for the help you need to enter the writing scene with grace and ease?

Now you can. This book is going to be your manual to perfect writing. Covering everything you need to know about research, execution, and production of any non fiction work you want to write.

You don't have to be a good writer to start this book, but no matter where you are now, by the end of this book you are going to be a great writer.

- Learn the tricks to effective research

- Learn how to gather and express your thoughts

- Learn how to avoid common mistakes beginners make

- Learn how to utilize what you are learning in the most effective way possible

- Learn how to become the writer you want to be

Table of Contents

Zach Raymond

Description

There are countless writers out there, all writing for different reasons. Some write for work, others write for school, and still others are aspiring writers just waiting for their big break into the world of literature.

No matter what the reason is for the writing, there is a common thread that pulls them all together. All writers seek to be good at what they do.

Are you one of these writers? Do you have a dream of publishing a great non fiction book? Or are you a student that has been challenged to write a research paper or thesis to make or break your grade?

Are you digging deep for the help you need to enter the writing scene with grace and ease?

Now you can. This book is going to be your manual to perfect writing. Covering everything you need to know about research, execution, and production of any non fiction work you want to write.

You don't have to be a good writer to start this book, but no matter where you are now, by the end of this book you are going to be a great writer.

- Learn the tricks to effective research

- Learn how to gather and express your thoughts

- Learn how to avoid common mistakes beginners make

- Learn how to utilize what you are learning in the most effective way possible

- Learn how to become the writer you want to be

Introduction

You may find the thought of a tortured writer hunched over their desk with a quill pen in hand to be one of the most romantic things you can imagine. The thought of Edgar Allen Poe or William Shakespeare with their adoring readers is a thought that can send shivers down your spine.

But, if you are a student that has been challenged with writing a research paper or if you have that non fiction book still hovering in the back of your mind and have no clue where to start, you are discovering that writing isn't nearly as romantic as you once thought.

That is, until you have that glorious breakthrough. That moment when you suddenly know what you want to say and how to say it, and what you put down on paper is both elegant and refined, informative yet conversational. All the walls that held you back now break down, and you are free to express yourself in any way you can imagine.

Now, the problem lies in getting you from point A to point B. You know what you want to write, you just aren't sure how to write it. Rest assured you have a great start. Just knowing what you want to write is a major step in the field of writing, but there are a lot of little steps that stand between you right now and having that finished manuscript in your hands.

The good news is that you can have that manuscript with just a little help from these pages, and in no time at all you are going to be that writer you are dreaming of being.

Let me erase all of the stress that hovers over an aimless writer's mind, and open the door for you. Enter into a world of creativity, expression, and originality as you allow your inner writer to come forth and take that pen in hand. By the time you reach the end of this book, you are going to have the confidence you need to write that piece you need to write, and submit to the world a masterpiece.

So what are you waiting for?

There is a writer inside all of us, they just need to be let out.

Chapter 1 – – An Approach to Non Fiction Writing

Non fiction is a branch of writing that has its pros and cons. For those that are writing a paper of some kind, this is the only option you have, but if you are writing a book, you have to think carefully before deciding on non fiction versus fiction.

The pros of the topic are obvious:

- non fiction writing is a collection of facts

- non fiction writing doesn't require the same kind of originality fiction writing does

- non fiction writing is largely inspired by research and experience

- non fiction writing can cover any topic on the planet

To name a few. Of course there are other benefits to writing non fiction, but don't forget there is always a drawback to a list of benefits.

So what are the cons?

- Non fiction writing is the highest targeted forms of writing to be subject to plagiarism

- Non fiction writing is based on fact, so a lot of research is required for any manuscript

- Non fiction writing must be based on fact

Although there are some obstacles that come into play when you are writing non fiction, you are going to find that it is also a very rewarding genre to write. The feeling of success you are going to experience when you see the response to what you have written is overwhelming, and something that is easy to become addicted to.

But, the most important part of a manuscript isn't so much what the topic is as how it is written. You can write about something fascinating but lose your audience due to poor writing skills, or you can write about something mundane but capture the attention of many because of your illustrious style.

But that's enough talking about writing, let's take the next step and actually learn how to write like a pro.

Plunge into the chapters to come to discover the key points of writing, and how to become the writer you have been dreaming about. You have what it takes inside of you, you just have to know how to use your skill.

Chapter 2 – Non Fiction Books

There was a time when writing a book was a dream that was hard to achieve. In this modern day, with the internet so readily available, book writing is becoming a very common activity.

Whether you are doing it to fulfill your dream, or if you are breaking into the writing industry for your job, there are still things you need to know for your book.

You can erase the idea that you are going to sit down and write the book start to finish right now. This is a lengthy process that takes time, effort, but most of all, research.

Mastering the Art of Research

Yes, research. The first thing you have to remember is when someone is reading your book, they are coming to your book for information. They want to learn about the topic you wrote about, and they want to come away from the book with the knowledge they need to accomplish what they want to accomplish.

This means it's your responsibility to give them the information they need. To do this, you have to give your readers facts, not opinions.

In order to give facts, you have to gather the facts effectively.

1. **Understanding what you Read** – You can't write a book or a paper if you don't understand what you are reading. The very first step to research is to understand what you are researching.

You might need to shop around for sources before you settle on the source for your paper. You need to understand what you are reading, and be able to effectively use the information that you read in the manuscript you are writing.

2. **How to think like a Researcher** – As a writer, you are going to have to take on the role of several different personas. The first is that of a researcher. If you can research well, you are going to cut the time you spend researching exponentially, and produce a better project in the end.

A researcher gathers information that is useful, and discards the rest.

So what is useful information?

- Information that directs people toward your end goal

- Information that backs up what you are talking about

- Information that furthers the knowledge you already have

- Information that is based on fact

- Information you can reference and cite, if need be

3. **Information Station**

- **Gathering Information** – Think of gathering information as plucking fruit off the vine. You want to take the best and leave the rest.

Any information that you don't need becomes filler words in your manuscript, and few things will cause more problems for you as a writer than filler words.

- **Leftovers** – There is a difference between useless information and left over information. Useless information is the information you shouldn't gather in the first place, left over information is the information that doesn't make it into your book.

This information is not useless, and odds are you are going to use it later on in life. Your best option for this kind of information is to file it away somewhere you can find it again later, and label it so you know what it is.

If you have ever seen a recipe catalogue, you have the right idea.

Selecting and Narrowing Your Topic

Another important thing you need to do is narrow your topic. Odds are if you are writing a paper or if you have been given a topic, you already know what your topic is, but there is a vast difference between "aquatic life" and "fish in the Amazon".

You need to be specific in your topic, and base your research on that particular topic.

Finding Sources

As I have already said, when you are gathering information, you need to use facts. This means that you need to use reliable sources. If you are writing on any topic, use a source that knows.

Never use tabloids for any information of any kind. Anything that is used for entertainment purposes need to be avoided when you are writing for useful information.

Look at the source of the site, if you don't find it obviously useful. For example, if you are writing a medical book or paper, WebMD is going to be a trusted source. However, if you are finding information off of someone's blog, the information you find may or may not be accurate.

It is your job as the author to produce information that is sound and reliable for your readers.

A Discussion on Length

Whether you are a freelance writer or a student, odds are you are dealing with a word count. Whether you are required to meet that count for your grade, or if you are reaching a word count for your client, you are going to have to be aware of how many words you are using.

This can be intimidating to some, which causes them to make a classic mistake... filler words. A filler word is a word that you don't need, adds nothing beneficial to the context, and is often painstakingly obvious.

To any reader, a filler word is going to stand out like a sore thumb. You might feel you are getting away with something, but your teacher is going to catch on quickly, and if you are working for someone you can bet they will pick up on those faster than anything else.

But how do I avoid filler words?

The best way to avoid these words is to use more information. Don't try to shirk on the information you are putting in your manuscript to cut back on work. Give it your all, and you won't have an issue. Another great way to avoid them is to use contractions.

If you use "don't" and "aren't" for the first half of your work, don't switch to "do not" or "are not" when you get closer to the end. This is not to say you can't use the proper form of the word, but if you are going to use it, use it throughout the book and not just towards the end.

Of course, these are guidelines you want to keep in mind no matter what kind of manuscript you are writing. Whether it is a book, a report, a paper, or anything else, you are going to benefit from this information.

I want you to read the next chapters with the same thing in mind, you can use this information for anything you are writing, although it may be more specific to what you are writing at the time.

A good writer knows how to use the information they gather and apply it to all sorts of different manuscripts they write. With practice, you are going to be able to do the same thing.

Chapter 3 – Research Papers

It doesn't matter if you are in grade school, high school, or college, the foundation of a research paper is the same. Of course, if you are in college you are going to have to rise to higher requirements than you would if you were in high school, but the core method you will use to accomplish the paper is going to be the same.

The research paper is informative. It answers questions that are asked, and it provides useful information to the person that is reading it. It doesn't matter what the person wants to learn from the paper, if it is well written, it needs to have factual information that is precise and accurate.

Taking Notes

Once you have the topic and the targeted word count for your paper in mind, you are ready to begin.

The first step is to gather information. If you know anything about the topic, feel free to add what you know to the paper, but be prepared to prove what you know.

As a rule of thumb, if you can't prove it, don't use it.

Proving is really easy if you are taking notes from trusted sources. Simply mention or briefly outline the method that was used to arrive at the conclusion, and you are set.

Of course, you'll have to cite the source of the information, but that isn't hard.

At first, take a lot of notes. Take notes like you are writing the entire book from the notes themselves. After you have all of the notes, you can go back through and decide what you are going to use and what you are going to save for later.

Remember, with each note you take, also make a note of the source from which it came. You have to cite your sources at the end of the paper, or you are going to be liable for the proof of the information yourself.

You can't write a paper and base it off of the notion "because I said so", you have to let your readers know you found information that is accurate and useful.

Another aspect to note taking you need to keep in mind is to scatter your sources. Make sure all of your sources are accurate, but don't put all of your eggs in one basket. Use a variety of sources and remember to cite them all.

First Drafts and Final Drafts

When it comes to a paper, a book, or any other manuscript, always assume you are going to write it at least three times.

Your first draft is like the preliminary. You jot down your ideas, you set up the basis of the paper, and you form the general idea of the layout of your paper. This is the time when you put your main ideas down on paper, you learn what notes you don't need, and you get a feel for the flow of the entire thing.

You don't have to worry so much about proper grammar or spelling at this point, although those things are always important. This is the rough draft, like a large chunk of earth that will later be formed into clay.

After your first paper, it is time to start polishing. Write the paper again, this time taking out the extra words that you don't want in there. Rephrase things to make them sound polished.

Check on grammar and spelling. Look at how you said certain things, and see if you can rearrange others to make them even better. Think of the second draft of your paper as sliding the pieces of the puzzle around to get them in the right place. Move and move again until you are happy with how the paper flows and what it says.

This is going to take some time. Don't rush it, although bear in mind any time restrictions you may have.

When you are happy with the flow of the second draft, you are now ready for the third and final draft.

(Keep in mind you are allowed as many drafts as you think you need, but you need to move towards better every time you revise.)

The final draft is your last hurrah. This is the point in which it all comes together, and you put out your best work. By the time you are at the end of the final draft, your work needs to be free of grammatical and spelling errors, the flow of the work needs to run smoothly, and your paper needs to convey the message you want it to convey.

Answer any questions that need to be answered, and remember to remove any of the filler words.

Citing Sources

Citing sources is a relatively easy thing to do, but all too many writers neglect to do it when they are finished with their papers. When you are finished with your paper, you have got to list the places you got the information.

To do this, you need to write the exact link from any website you used, or you need to list the name of the book, the author of the book, and the page number from which you got the information.

In this modern age, you are likely to use more sources from the internet than you are from an actual paper book, but it is still important to know how to cite the sources from paperback work. Just remember that even when you cite the sources you used, you still have to avoid plagiarism at all cost.

In the chapters to come, we are going to take a look at plagiarism and how to avoid it, but for now, just remember to keep note of all of the sources you use, and list them at the end of your work.

Chapter 4 – Mastering the Theses

The thesis is the main point of what your paper is talking about. A research paper has a point, but it may or may not have a thesis. When you are writing a paper, you are conveying an idea, and your thesis is the main point of this idea... or, better said... the idea itself.

The biggest mistake students make when they are writing a thesis is to hide the thesis in the paper. They bury it with loads of information that side tracks the reader, or they babble on and on then squish the thesis in at the very end.

These are both poor methods when it comes to your thesis. When you are writing a thesis, you want it to be clear, out in the open, and bold.

The thesis is brief, only one or two sentences, but it states the purpose of your entire paper.

Where do I put the thesis statement?

The placement of the thesis statement depends on the length of your paper. If you are writing a shorter paper, place it early on... in the introduction or even as the first sentence.

If you are writing a longer essay, place it in the second paragraph. You want to keep this towards the front of your paper because your thesis statement is going to say what the point of your paper is, and give your reader a sense of direction.

Here are a few examples of how to create a revised and concise thesis statement:

First, the poor example:

- There are serious objections to violence in modern day movies.

This is loose, broad, and open to a lot. While you can write a paper based on this thesis statement, there are so many better ways to say what you want to say that revise and reduce the statement into a more concise statement.

- The violence in modern day movies is causing a lot of issues with the youth of this country.

- The blood and gore in modern day films degrades men and women and reduces them to images of what people should be.

- The lack of emotion in the modern day film is painfully obvious compared to the same kind of films showed twenty or thirty years ago.

As you can see, the first statement can get the job done, but the latter three statements give you an actual basis for your paper. You can build off of each of them in specific ways that conveys to your reader what you are trying to say.

Make sure Your Thesis Statement is Specific

You want your thesis statement to be short and to the point. When you have written your statement, take a moment and analyze what you have written. Ask yourself if it is short and to the point, or if you have added in more words than there needed to be.

Ask: "Did I settle on a single point with this statement?"

Check: "Am I using proper and concise grammar in joining my statement?"

Remember: "My statement is the point of my paper. Is this what I want to say to my readers?"

If you are finding contradictions in your thesis from any of these questions, rewrite your thesis to better fit with the answers. A loose thesis is going to convey scattered thoughts and leave your reader wondering where you are going with the paper, a thesis that has multiple points is going to cause confusion later on, and a thesis that isn't what you want your paper to be about is a misplaced thesis.

No matter what your paper is about, what you want to say to your readers, or what you hope to accomplish with your entire paper, you have got to make it all shine through with your thesis statement.

When you have your point in mind, make that the forefront of your paper, and build the rest of your paper off of that.

Three Key Points to Writing a Killer Thesis Statement

You don't have to make random stabs in the dark to create an awesome thesis statement. There are general rules you can follow that are going to make your thesis statements short, to the point, and ready to convey your idea.

These rules are:

• Avoid the use of technical terms. If you aren't writing an actual technical paper, avoid the technical jargon. This includes slang, terms related to a particular job, or common clichés of the day. When you are writing a thesis statement, say what you want to say, only that, and that in its fullest.

• Don't every use vague words. "exciting", "interesting", "somewhat", and so on and so forth are vague words that don't illicit any real response from your readers any more than reading a recipe would have an effect on a small child.

When you are writing your thesis statement, you need to make it open, clear, and relatable to anyone that is reading it.

- In addition to vague words, you need to avoid words that are abstract. Words that are broad, such as 'culture' and 'society' are words that remove the reader from any real responsibility to the content of the paper, so avoid those.

You want your readers to relate to what you are saying, and you want to have an effect on them after they read it. To do this, you have to write statements that engage them, that pull them close, and grab their attention.

You are going to learn as a writer that you can have an incredible effect on the readers of your work with the use of the right words.

How to Keep the Focus of Your Thesis Statement

The worst thing you can do to your reader is to confuse them with your thesis. To avoid doing this, you need to know what you want to say yourself. If you are given the topic of a paper, it is rare that you are told what to say, so this is something you need to figure out on your own.

Once you know what you want to say, think of the most concise way you can say it. Condense the statement down into the shortest way possible, and don't use words that aren't necessary.

While a thesis paper sounds really intimidating when you are given the project, it doesn't have to be. You can conquer the thesis statement in a matter of minutes if you are dedicated to it, and you'll never struggle with another thesis paper again.

Chapter 5 – How to Avoid a Dissertation Disaster

For many students, the dissertation is the pinnacle of dread. There are times when the entire grade for the class rests on the student's ability to write a good dissertation, and for those that don't know what they are doing, this assignment feels like a gunshot.

There is good news, however, and that is the fact dissertations can be conquered with a few key tricks that you can easily achieve. You are going to have to put in the work, so I am not going to say this is an easy thing to do, but I will assure you that it is more than doable if you are willing to put in the effort.

What is a Dissertation?

A dissertation is a lengthy essay on a particular subject. It argues in the defense of a stated thesis, and more often than not it is used by students going for their doctorate.

The downside to these papers is that you are going to be graded by those that have managed to pass before, which isn't as easy as you would think. The key to this success is to persevere over them, and with the right paper, you can.

How to Properly Approach a Dissertation Paper

The first thing you need to do is approach your paper with the confidence you are going to do well. The more you dread the paper, and the more nervous you are about writing it, the harder it is going to be to write a good one.

With that in mind, keep these key things as your main strategy when writing the paper:

- The two things you need to aim for in your dissertation are 'originality' and 'substance'. Keeping it brief is going to be your downfall with your dissertation.

Make it substantial, give your readers something to read, something to think about, and something to learn. You can't just pass this off as a 'good enough' or something like that. You really do have to give it your all and aim for the stars.

- A dissertation is more than a thesis. You need to focus on lessons that were learned rather than just the facts that support what you are talking about. Make it personal. Show how you are going to apply what you have learned and how it has effected the course you are taking.

- Critical thinking is the name of the game in your dissertation. There is to be no speculation, no curiosity, no guess work. You need to think about what you want to say, lead your readers in light of what you want them to think, and answer their questions in your paper.

You are in control of the outcome of your writing of this paper, so don't get mystical or try to pull of an imaginary scenario with your readers. Tell them the facts and guide them towards the outcome.

• Remember that sources are of essence when it comes to your dissertation. You have absolutely got to point back to where you found the information, ensure it is accurate and able to be used, and keep your information to the basics.

Don't be redundant, and don't be overtly detailed. The point of a dissertation is to give a lot of good information. Not a lot of words that don't really say a lot in the end.

- Each and every sentence in your dissertation needs to be correct in a grammatical sense. I can't emphasize enough how important it is to have excellent grammar and proper spelling throughout.

Even one poor usage of a word, or a single misspelled word could cost you dearly. This is because these are little details that you are going to have to pay attention to in your line of work, and they are going to think if you can't do it with a paper, how are you going to do it on the field?

When you are writing this paper, don't rush. If you are on a time limit, schedule so you can get the most out of the time you have, and do your research thoroughly. Your entire grade depends on it, so treat this project as though you believe that to the core.

Use Your Dissertation to Learn, and as Proof of Your Learning

One of the main points of the dissertation is to cause the student to think. They want you to prove what you have learned, show them you can learn and study and think clearly on a subject, and that you can deepen your thinking to overcome problems.

Think of this as a challenge you can conquer, and a chance to show the world that you are ready to face what is coming next. All too many students get bogged down with the details of the dissertation that they forget the point of it in the first place.

You can do it, you are a good writer, and you just need the direction and the motivation to show them what you got. Now that you know what it takes to write a good dissertation, there is nothing standing in your way.

Science and Sources

Remember that each sentence you use in your dissertation must be both logical and able to be scientifically proven. There isn't to be any speculation or anything far-fetched in the content of the book.

Stating sources is going to be second nature with this paper. It is so important that you show where you got the information that you should check, double check, and even triple check your sources before you submit the work as finished.

You are going to submit this work to some of the toughest people you can imagine, so don't mess around with the facts you are using.

This all sounds intimidating, I know. Here is a word of advice, however, to how you can succeed in this realm. Don't give up. Take this advice as a challenge to push you to your fullest potential. You are able to put out all of this information as you have learned it already, you just have to prove that you know it.

Follow the same guidelines as with a research paper. Write, re-write, and proofread before you submit. Don't be afraid to edit, remove, and add in things where you feel it is necessary, and show your readers what you are capable of.

With a lot of work, and dedication, you are going to write a killer dissertation, and get a great grade when you finally submit it to your readers.

Chapter 6 – The Most Common Mistakes Beginning Writers Make and How to Avoid Them

As a writer, it is tempting to jump in and give it all you have. That, of course, has its pros and cons, but you have to remember that there is a right and wrong way to do it. There are always mistakes that you can make, and there are ways to avoid these mistakes if you are careful.

My goal with this book is to help you learn how to become a better writer, and to do this, I am going to show you the common mistakes a lot of people make and how to avoid those mistakes.

The Problem of Plagiarism

Plagiarism is by far the biggest issue that writers face. It can be easy to do it by trying, and it is easier than you think to do it without trying. This is because there are a lot of rules that come into play when it comes to plagiarism that a lot of people don't understand.

When you are writing, or taking notes, or using quotes, you can't use the direct quote without citing the source. If you are able to use the direct quote, make sure you use the source of who said it and where you got it. You can't just say it, or say that a person said it, without using the quote for them.

You absolutely cannot copy actual paragraphs and use them in your paper even if you cite the source. When you are getting information from the paragraph, get the main point of the paragraph and leave it at that.

Of course, even when you are only using the main idea you still need to cite the source, but there is a difference between using the main point of the paragraph and actually using the paragraph.

Again, there are different rules when it comes to different kinds of writings. When you are writing cookbooks, you have to be really careful when it comes to recipes that are online. You have to change a lot about a recipe before you can use it in your book, and you can't just cite the source and call it good.

Before you write a book, check into the specifics of the copyright laws before you begin. There are a lot of different laws or rules that are easy to find, you just have to do an internet search if you are really uncertain as to what they are.

Plagiarism can be hard to get used to, but once you are, creating your own content is going to come as second nature.

Proof Reading and Editing

Following plagiarism, the next biggest mistake you could possibly make as a writer is skipping the final read through of your work. You have no idea how much credibility you can lose with a reader if you are speaking on a topic with a paper that is riddled with grammatical and spelling errors.

Yes, proofreading is boring, yes it is mundane. Yes there are a lot of things you would rather be doing, especially when you think you got it all right the first time around, but it is a step that is going to really save you a lot of pain later on down the road when you hear the feedback on your work.

Believe me, you may not hear how awesome your paper is written if it is written well, but you will surely hear about the mistakes that you made if you fail to proofread or edit your work before you publish it.

Your number one rule when it comes to editing and proofreading is:

Remember the spell check button is a tool, not a cure all.

In other words, this is a system with flaws. Yes, it will ensure all the words are spelled correctly, but that doesn't mean that you used the right word in the right context.

"There" is spelled correctly in that sense, but also in the sense of "their" and "they're". Your spell check is going to bypass all three of these, although if one is used improperly you will still get knocked for a mistake, even though it was spelled correctly.

So by all means, run the spell check, but only use that as an assistant to your editing, and never as your only means of proofreading.

Under Revision versus Over Revision

I hope by now I have instilled the fear of all things sacred into you about editing and revising, but with that in mind I want to also let you know you *can* overdue it.

I know that sounds strange, with all of the emphasis that I put on editing and removing the parts of your paper that don't belong, but while you are editing away, remember to use common sense.

You need to have a complete paper when you are finished, so don't hack it down to just a few sentences. Write your paper to say what you need it to say, and leave it at that. There doesn't have to be all of the extra shininess to add to the affect if you write well and keep your point plain and simple.

Keep it in balance, and you won't lose your readers, but neither will you bore them with unnecessary reading.

Unhelpful Sources

Writers aren't the only group plagued with the dread of unhelpful sources, but they are certainly on the forefront of the group.

There are few things more frustrating than wasting your time. When you are in the research process, you want to get the information you need, and get out of there. After all, who wants to spend hours reading what others have written when you yourself want to be on your computer writing your own manuscript?

Or, if you are just trying to get a good grade for a class, research is little more than a bother when you know you have to get it all written and edited before you can turn it in.

With this being said, avoiding unhelpful sources is a must.

These are the places that are going to waste your time, give you poor information, or require a lot out of you before they allow you to reach the information you need to continue.

These are a few examples of these sources, but there are more besides theses so use your head when you are browsing the internet:

• Online magazines. They ask for your information, throw tons of ads in your face, and give you little of what you really need. Avoid them.

- Online forums. These are the chat rooms for people to give the most confusing and contradictory information without ever arriving at a single conclusion.

- Open source websites. If you have the option to edit what you are reading online, take what you read with a grain of salt. If anyone can say anything, then *anyone* can say *anything*.

- Tabloids. We all know the reputation, and it's there for a reason.

- Word of mouth. When writing something that is going to be critiqued, always use credible, real sources. He said she said doesn't belong in any manuscript.

And of course you could add to this list. The bottom line is: If a source is not backed with actual fact or knowledge, walk away from it and find another site that is.

Chapter 7 – Getting Back to the Basics

While I wanted to make a point of listing the common mistakes you should avoid, I wasn't going to leave you hanging with the list of what not to do. For everything you shouldn't do with your paper, there is something that you should do lurking in the shadows, just waiting to get out.

I know in addition to proofreading and editing the other thing people dread doing is reviewing the basics, but these are important, and as a writer, you have to know the answers if you want to have a prayer of making it in the genre.

Review the Parts of Speech

We were in grade school when we learned the eight parts of speech, but unfortunately, many people lose interest in them and what they are shortly thereafter.

And once out of high school, the knowledge of the parts of speech fades all together.

Here they are listed now, study them and use them properly in your paper.

Noun

Names a person, place, thing, or idea (dog, house, man, America)

Pronoun

Takes the place of a noun in a sentence (he, I, him, them, her)

Adjective

Describes the noun (hot, cold, red, fat)

Verb

An action word (run, sit, play, write)

Adverb

Describes a verb, and usually ends in -ly (quickly, hotly, arrogantly, gently)

Prepositions

Links a noun to another word in the sentence (to, at, on, over)

Conjunctions

A joining word, can join sentences, clauses, or words (and, but, nor, when)

Interjections

Short exclamations found in sentences that add feeling to the sentence (ouch! Oh! Hi!)

Any writer ought to be able to rattle off the parts of speech, as well as state what each part is if they intend to be a good writer. This is not to say that you can't write if you don't know what the parts of speech are, but you are going to be so much better if you know what they are and what they do before you attempt to write your manuscript.

If you want to take it to the next level, I recommend you enroll in an online class on the basics of grammar and proper usage. There are countless free classes all over the internet, and while they aren't necessarily accredited for any college work, you are still getting the information you need to write a good paper.

Chapter 8 – Publication

If you are writing a thesis or a research paper, it is likely you will hand in your work in class and that will be the end of that. If you, however, are taking your book from a manuscript on your paper to having it published, there are certain things you need to know before you attempt such a project.

For starters, you have to decide if you are going to hire a publisher, or if you are going to do the publishing yourself. There are pros and cons to both, so make sure you look into both sides before you make your final decision.

Regardless of how you are getting your manuscript published, you do have to follow certain rules.

From Planning to Production

The first thing you need to do is plan the work. If you are writing a book with publication as the end goal (which is very likely the case if you are undertaking the actual writing of a book), you are going to want to have a schedule to follow.

You don't have to be highly detailed in your planning, you just have to give your publisher a general idea of when and where your book is going to be. List where you are in your writing at certain times, where you plan to be at a given time, and what you plan to do with the book when you are done.

List how you want it published, how you are going to market, and how you want it to look when finished. This is ultimately your work, but you do have to keep the other people you are working with in the loop of how you are doing things.

The plan is like the first draft of your work. You have a rough idea of what you want to do, but you may have to revise a few times before it actually reaches production.

Project Management

Essentially, you plan the work, then you work the plan. In the project planning, you listed how and where you wanted to be at given points in time. Under the project management, you are making that happen.

You can do this all yourself, or you can hire a manager to do this for you. Keep in mind publishing is an investment, and the more you pay for, the harder it is going to be to pay yourself back. If you have more money than time, hire away. But if you happen to be short on the cash end, try to do as much of this as you can yourself.

It does take time and effort, but the money you are going to save in the long run, in addition to the fact you can make it exactly as you want it is going to make it a lot more worth it than hiring someone to do the work for you.

Building the Story Board

Both fiction and non fiction books have story boards. A story board is merely the projected flow of the book. How you lead from one topic into another, where you want to begin, and where you want to finish.

For fiction writers, they will often draw pictures to determine where and why things happen, but as a non fiction writer, you just need to make minor notes on the how's and the why's things are the way they are. When you are in the actual writing of the book you can adjust as necessary, but this is your first guide in the basic beginnings of the book.

Progress Review

Progress reviews depend on the size of the project. You can do this yourself, or you can have someone else do it, all depending on what you want. If you are working as a writer for someone else, you may be asked to produce a project review, and if that is the case, all you have to do is let them know where you are on the work.

Sometimes they ask to see the work, which is also simple, just make sure they understand that it is the first draft of the work and not the final copy. This is going to save them a lot of stress and you a lot of explaining than if you were to submit the work as is!

Publishing

When you come to the publishing itself, there are a few ways you can do this. Amazon has its own self-publishing section that will walk you through the process, but if you have a publisher, you don't have to worry about any of this.

Remember no matter what you do there are going to be contracts to sign and deals to make, and all of this is a leap of faith in hopes the book is going to do well.

Just remember, the better the quality of the book, the better it is going to do on the market. A well-written, highly informative book is going to do a lot better than a book that was just tossed together with poor information. You get the same effort you put into it, so don't shirk.

I hope you were able to learn everything you needed in this book to make your own manuscript a success. Remember to follow the guidelines that I put in place, and that you read and re-read what you have written before you turn it in for review.

You are a great writer, and you can produce a book that is going to make a difference to those that are reading it, you just have to back your knowledge with skills.

Conclusion

There you have it, everything you need to know about non fiction writing, and everything you need to get started with your writing project today. I know there is a large mix of excitement as well as nerves as you take on this new project, but you can't let yourself get overwhelmed.

The most important thing you need to remember is to take your time. If you are on a time limit (a deadline for a class, for example) you are going to need to stick with the project plan a lot closer than if you are writing for the fun of it, but either way you have to read and re-read what you wrote.

Be critical of your work, but never too hard on yourself. You need to challenge yourself, but encourage yourself as well. Do your best and apply what you learn, and always be willing to learn more, to be better, and to achieve more.

You will surprise yourself at the creativity you have inside of you, and when you finish that manuscript, and see it turned in and graded well or your book published for the first time, you are going to have that sense of achievement that you can't get anywhere else.

There is great excitement when you finally feel like a writer, no matter what it is you are writing. That is what this book is about, and exactly what I want you to achieve. Unleash that inner writer, and let the creativity flow from the ink in your pen.

Get ready to put your thoughts down on paper, and express yourself among the writers in the world.

Other Books By Author

One Hour Trading:

Make Money With a Simple Strategy, One Hour Daily

Investing For Beginners:

Rules To Make Money Investing Like A Pro - The Ultimate Beginner's Guide on How To Get Rich Trading

Sales:

The art Of Selling – How To Make Anyone say YES

Stocks:

Stock Trading For Beginners: The Ultimate Beginner's Guide - Everything You Need To Know To Get You Started On The Stock Market

Project Management:

The Ultimate Beginner's Guide To Manage Any Project - Managing Projects Like the Professionals

Small Business

25+ Tips for Starting and Running a Small Business Successfully

How to Analyze People:

Reading People 101: A Guide With 25+ Tricks To Read The Person You Are Talking To

Influence And Persuasion

A Guide With 25+ Tricks To Influence and Persuade The Person You Are Talking To

Can I Ask A Favor?

If you enjoyed this book, found it amazing or otherwise then I'd really appreciate it if you would post a short review on Amazon. I do read all the reviews personally so that I can continually write what people are wanting.

Thank you for your support!